Dancing With Depression

Tom Atkins

ISBN:1537789821
ISBN-13: 978-1537789828

DEDICATION

You never dance alone. This book is dedicated to the therapists, pastors, friends and families who have stood beside me and helped me find my way. And to the love of my life, Cindy Mertzic, who has brought me more joy than I probably deserve

CONTENTS

Forward

I want to start this book at the end. Or at least in the middle.

I mean, depression is not one of those things that people are jumping up and down to read about. After all, it's so… depressing.

But it also affects a ton of us. I had no idea how many until I began my own fight over a decade ago.

My fight? It has been hard. Painful. Ugly. Never ending. You will learn more about that later in this book. But right this minute, as I write this……

… I am at the Relentlessly Cheerful Diner, a favorite spot of mine, a cup of coffee at my side. The cook is rustling up an omelet and sautéed spinach for me. I have a couple of pieces of copywriting to do this morning. Easy work. Good work for a good client.

Earlier today, I took my son to school. He was bright and cheerful and had plans for the afternoon. We talked about music and theatrical lighting, a particular love of his. I smiled as I dropped him off, quietly rejoicing at how he has blossomed since moving up with me about a year ago.

After letting him off, I drove here. Inside the car, there is still a faint whiff of perfume from the last visit with the woman I love. I had to smile. I feel particularly blessed by her, someone I can talk to so freely and safely it is like talking to myself, someone who encourages me when sometimes, I have trouble encouraging myself. She is a constant joy. Truly.

Yeah, life is good. Not perfect, but good.

After all, I still battle depression daily. I have my days when I don't want to crawl out of bed, when I feel flat, when enjoying life is hard. But they are less now than at any point in the last decade and a half. There is stuff to do on the house and the cars need work. I struggle with being good enough. I always feel I can do more, even if that is not always the case. I have the same health problems and money problems and other issues most everyone else has. There's no Camelot in this life, I can tell you. But all in all, life is good.

Why am I writing this?

Part of it is because it seems a miracle to me that I can say, honestly that life is good. I spent so much time in the black hole of my depression, that I assumed that was where I would stay forever. You may have felt the same way. Or someone you know has felt that way. To be in this good place is a breathtaking. I called it a miracle. It is. And part of this book is my celebration of that miracle.

But part of it is to let others know there is a path out. It can get better. It's worth the fight Even when we don't win entirely, we can win a lot. We can gain much of our joy again, and it's magnificent. And if I can crawl back, as broken as I was, anyone can do it.

Not alone of course. Science and experience have pretty much proved we can't get through depression alone. I got through with a cast of characters ranging from therapists, pastors, friends who listened and learned and encouraged me while I fought the battle, both physical and emotional. No, we don't dig out of our black hole alone.

Not easily either. It's work. Work when we don't feel like working. Work that is sometimes painful. Work that for a while seems to be doing little good. I'll never be cured. I'll always be battling. That's not a bad thing. It's just the reality.

And certainly not instantly. The medications don't fix everything. They just make it better so we can do the hard work of putting our brain in its place. They are a step, and there are many steps. It will take years. Not it might take years, it WILL take years ,

But stick with it, Fight the battle day in and day out and there's an incredible reward ahead of you. Joy. Strength. Confidence. Personal Power. And an enjoyment of life that once was lost.

This book began as a series of posts on my Quarry House Blog (www.quarryhouse.wordpress.com). When I began this it a year or so ago, I got a lot of feedback. Most were kind – talking about how it helped. Some though were negative – accusing me of wanting the world to feel sorry for me and in effect telling me to shut up.

But shutting up is the wrong thing to do. If we live in darkness and don't share, no one will know. No one will help. We will not get better. Battles are not fought alone. Or rather, battles that we win are not fought alone.

So my friends, fight the fight. Gather your army. Know the war is long.

But also know there is beauty on the other side. Amazing, joy and beauty. Trust me on this one. I've been there. And this is my story.

Be well. Travel wisely,

Tom

DECLARATION OF WAR

You light one in the morning,
and then another,
at first to keep the dark at bay,
but as the light gathers,
and pushes the blackness away,

each flicker becomes something more
than survival.
It becomes
a declaration of war.

About this poem

I can remember early in my war with depression, telling my
therapist "I don't want to survive depression, I want to shine
again."

"You can," she told me. "Are you ready for war?"

HARD WORK

I was in Washington DC a few days ago and the headset to my phone died, so I made a trip to Best Buy to pick up a new one. When you travel like I do, a headset is a must.

The clerk was a young man from India. There was something wrong with one hand, a handicap of some sort that left the hand still and useless, but he deftly ran the register and bagged my earbuds. Noticing I was from Vermont, he told me of a summer he had spent here, and how much he loved it, how he hope to go back. It was a slow morning and we talked for about twenty minutes, our conversation running from Vermont to travel in general to local restaurants and jazz.

He was active the whole time we talked, cleaning up the register area, putting things in order, always productive even in the midst of our conversation. At one point he fumbled something slightly with his still hand, and he never skipped a beat, catching the item with his good hand. "It is trouble sometimes." he said " This hand."

"You do remarkably well." I said.

He smiled. "Thank you for noticing. It is hard work having a still hand. People don't see that."

I have thought about that conversation over the past few days, as the news has unfolded about Robin Williams' death. There has been a great deal of talk about his struggles with depression and substance abuse over the years. And then the latest revelation of his early onset of Parkensons. If anything good has come out of the tragedy of his death, it has been the depth of discussion on depression, it's causes and how pervasive it is.

My conversation with the young clerk at Best Buy has had me thinking about an aspect of Depression that I have not heard much about however. One that deserves understanding.

Depression is hard work.

I was diagnosed with Depression as I was going through a divorce nearly a decade and a half ago. Sometimes depression is situational and goes away as the situation gets better. I had experienced that situational depression twenty years ago during a long, slow recovery from viral pneumonia. As my health came back, my depression healed as well.

But the Depression that came a decade and a half ago moved in to stay. It has never left me. At times it's a little better. At times it's a little worse. But it is never gone.

I function fine. I get my work done. I manage to write and preach and paint. My house is kept up. The bills get paid and the grass gets cut. I go to movies and galleries and savor good meals and good company.

But it's work. When you fight depression, everything about life is work. Even the easy stuff.

Getting out of bed in the morning is work. Everything in my body and mind just wants to stay there all day. Simple things like calling the DMV and washing the dishes take a serious act of will to begin. I can remember before the depression. These things were not work. You just did them automatically. There was no effort of will to do them.

These days, and for the last decade and a half, it's been like pushing a huge boulder up hill to do everything. In regular life, there were times I had to push the boulder up hill and times it rolled down hill on its own. Inertia took over at a certain point and things became easier But with depression there is no inertia. Everything you do is pushing up hill. Even staying still has the weight of that boulder threatening to roll back over you.

I am far more disciplined than I used to be. I take medication regularly and monitor my moods so I am taking the right amount (more or less) as my body needs. I have a counselor who keeps me on track. I used to be far more spontaneous in my schedule, but these days I keep to a regular schedule which helps. I go to bed at a regular time most nights, which helps.

But still, it's work. Every. Single. Thing, is work, a lot of work. Like the young clerk, I work hard to make it seem effortless. But of course, that's more work

Every now and then, I surrender. When I have a a day with no responsibilities, I don't get up. This is not the normal lazy morning, but a surrender to a mind that lies to me in its depression, that tells me I can't do this. And I just surrender. It's not really good to do this, except for one thing.

It's a day of rest. A day of not fighting this disease and it's insidious lies of what you can and can not do.

And then I begin again.

I don't talk about it much. I don't want people to feel any more sorry for me than if I had any other chronic sickness. Truly, I am glad I CAN fight it. For some people the Depression is so bad that they can't fight it.The Depression wins again and again. But for me, at the end of a productive day, when I am savoring a bit of cheese, or a piece of fresh bread, or a small glass of wine, there is a huge sense of victory that I did not have before the depression.

I have fought the beast today And I won.

We all know people who fight Depression. I see statistics like one out of ten pretty regularly, so that's likely about right. Some of them we are aware of and some we don't see it. They work hard, harder than you know, to just function. They are not weak, as society sometimes portrays them, but far stronger than they should have to be. And often far more tired. They fight each day to function, to claim the joys in their life. And often, we hide it so well, like the young clerk, that no one notices.

But if you do? It's OK to acknowledge it. The young clerk's face lit up. He had been seen. As a person, whole and victorious, his work and victory acknowledged and seen. When we are seen, not just the depression, but the life we've battled to claim, it gives us a sense of our own victory to know others see our battle and that we have done well.

Off my soapbox. Time to get back to work.

Tom

THE MOST COURAGEOUS PEOPLE

When I was in my early forties I had an automobile accident. I was T-boned in my little car and both of my arms dislocated. Popped completely out of the socket. The EMT's popped them back in, and I began about a year of physical therapy.

I was fortunate in that my job at the time had me traveling and often staying in pretty decent hotels, complete with exercise rooms. Weights and rowing machines, several times a week were part of my routine. (I hate weights)

People were very solicitous. They were nice. They told me how good I was to stay with the rehab work for the full cycle of the year. They knew how much I hated it (though I eventually grew to like the rowing machine – very zen).

Fast forward till after my divorce. I was in a funk that lasted a couple of years. Actually it wasn't a funk. It was depression and probably I was in it even before the divorce.

For those of you who don't have depression, or haven't really looked into it, there are all kinds of physical reasons people might have it. It can come from a slow change in the brain's chemistry, and it can come from emotional trauma so strong that it physically changes the brain.

The same is true of other mental illnesses, be they anxiety, depression, or a whole gamut of things. Our brains lie to us. They tell us things are worse than they are, that they are darker than they are, that we have less worth than we do, that we are unloveable.

Like my dislocated shoulders, there was work to do. I was put on medication. I had therapy to do. A lot of it.

The thing about therapy is that you can't predict going in how long it will take, or how hard it will be. It's an act of faith, really – faith that you have a good therapist, faith that the process will work, faith that it's worth the pain and work (and it is painful and it is work. I'd rather lift weights any day.). You have to believe, despite the evidence of the first few months or year, that you are going to come out on the other side in a far better, far stronger place.

There's a difference too in how people see physical illness and mental/emotional illness, and how they treat the people with it. People feel shame about mental illness in a way they don't about physical things, and society perpetuates that. People are put down for their weakness when the issue is mental/emotional while they are always supportive of physical problems. When we are injured, everyone wants to know what happened, how they can help. When our hearts and minds are broken, we avoid the subject.

The medical system is the same way. I have diabetes. As long as I live, my insurance will pay for the medicine I take each day. It will pay for the regular doctors' visits I have to make every six months or so, for as long as I live. People tend to live a long time in my family, and I am doing my best to follow in their footsteps.

But have a mental issue? Most plans give you six months or so of mental health care. Some don't even treat it at all. Consider that it often takes years to completely get back on track and get our brain in a truly healthy place and that means you end up paying a lot of money beyond insurance to get well again. (I spent over three years with my counselor in Virginia and followed up with a counselor here in Vermont for a year and a half.).

That's insanity in my mind. Consider the cost of having so many people suffering mentally/emotionally. Lost productivity. Broken relationships. Crime (how many of the mass shooters in the last year had serious, untreated mental issues), Drugs. All with untreated mental illnesses they can't afford care for. But they can get their diabeties, or other chronic medications every month.

But I won't ever change that system. I'm not a politician, or someone with enough money or influence to change politics. I'm just a guy.

What I do hope I can change, for just a few people, is how we see those who are suffering from these things and have chosen to fight it. Those who, despite a society and a medical system that treats them as "off", not "ill". Those who have the faith, and the courage to not just take a pill, but do the real work that has a far better chance of bringing us back to health, despite knowing that real work is going to be hard, and scary, and has not real timetable to get us back to another place.

These people are the strongest, most courageous people I know. My admiration for them is beyond words. They may seem broken, but they are people of incredible faith and courage. Maybe it is because I have made the journey that i feel so strongly that those who fight to reclaim the truth of their goodness are amazing, but what ever the reason I know one thing.

They are my heros.

Be well. Travel wisely.

Tom

AN OPEN LETTER

Good evening my friend.

Oh, you're a pretty lousy friend, I'll give you that. You lie to me at every turn, and you never have anything positive to say. You really should have killed me when you had a chance, when I was so broken down and weak and confused and hurt. You could have. Heaven knows you have done others in. Lots of them. Oh, you never got on the death certificate, but any of us who know you knew who the culprit was.

I have to give you an "A" for persistence. It's been well over a decade now since you took over parts of my brain. short circuited my joy and began having your way with me. And you've hung in there the whole time. No matter what I do, you are right there lurking, waiting for that next opportunity to whack away at me. That persistence has been hard for me to deal with. At heart, I am a simple guy. I just want to do my writing and art, do my work, love the people dear to me. Simple stuff. I like life simple.

You have robbed me of that simplicity. I have to look at every negative thought to make sure it's legit or not (some are, after all.). I have to look at every emotion too, to see which ones are just feelings, and which ones are you lurking with your dagger-like lies. Every thought. Every emotion. Do you have any idea how exhausting that can be?

And here you've snuck up on me again. My fault. I let my guard down. Things were cruising along so nicely. I got sloppy. I took my medication, but I forgot that is only part of the armor. I got comfortable. And you snuck right in. It had been so long, months maybe, that I began to believe you had surrendered.

But you never do, do you? You snuck back in and for a while, I wasn't sure what was wrong. I just knew something was. It took me a while to recognize you. Hard to imagine, isn't it? After twelve or fourteen years, you'd think I'd know you as well as I know myself.

That's OK. I'm on to you now. The armor's back on and I'll beat you back like I have every other time.

I wasn't kidding though, when I called you my friend. Because of you, I've grown stronger. I had to. I've grown more mindful. I had to. I know myself way better than I ever had any intention of. I probably know my good sides and my flaws better than anyone alive. even those who have been your allies. I've learned to open up, to share my struggle and guess what? People get it. They have shared their love and propped me up when I needed it, Ha! And all that time you told me to be ashamed. I've regained my spirituality, thanks to you, and even if I was as weak as you make me out to be, the big guy always wins.

Yes, it's a lot more work dealing with you and making sure you're back in your cage day in and day out. I get tired of sticking the muzzle on you every morning. But doing it day in and day out has made me stronger. I know your moves and you haven't introduced a new lie in years and years. I pretty much know them by heart now, and when I hear them…. I know who's talking. And it's not me. And it's certainly not truth.

So back into the cage with you. Yes, I know you slink out every night. But I also know what I did not know for so long. You're a coward. You're a bully. You can't stand up to the truth. You can't stand up to those who fight back. You only win when people surrender. And when I am diligent, and waggle my sword, you slink back where you belong.

Nice try though. I would say better luck next time, but there's no luck involved. It's got nothing to do with you. You've thrown your worst at me. You don't get weaker, but I am getting stronger. And I will keep getting stronger. You have made me become tougher than you. I have reasons to live. People who love me. Good work yet to do. Joy, yes you heard me right, joy to experience.

So deal with it. I'll see you again in the morning, sword in hand. I'll enjoy seeing you skulk.

Tom

KILLING FROM THE EDGES

At dusk you see him,
a dark shadow against the bright lights
that deign to ward off the night,
a reminder
that every moment, you are stalked,
that he waits to pull you into the night,
to make you his prisoner
forever.

But not tonight,
not while you stand in the light
of fire, of love, not as long as your sword is at the ready,
and those that love you most
stand at your side.

For the shadow is a coward,
a bully, stalking in darkness,
fearful of the light, killing from the edges,
afraid of truth, light,
and most of all, the vulnerable power of love.

About this poem

Depression. The Devil. The demons within. The evil without. Sin. This could be about any and all of those.

And about love, of course. Always about love.

Tom

A REFUSAL TO DIE

Go ahead, try.
Starve me to death
with silence,
a dry desert,
harsh, only the sound
of the wind,
of my own voice
echoing through the canyon,
a cry for help, lost in the night,
foreign, like a Gregorian Chant,
both beautiful and intelligible,
a thing of the past, haunting
but no more understandable
than the death of love.

Watch me whither,
slowly gasping,
a dry voice, hungry for an ear,
lost, but always searching,
my song less a dirge
than a determined mantra,
a movie score of suffering and growth
that plays low and soft,
but stronger than you can understand.

Watch me grow,
for my roots run deeper than you can imagine,
deep, thin veins stretching
both to heaven and to hell,
feeding off both,
finding reason to live,
to believe, to fight past the dry night,
to create my own spring,
to defy the barren winter,
to live,
not simply, merely
survive.

DISCIPLINE

I wrote a poem this morning. But then, I write a poem every morning. It's part of my routine when I get up. I meditate, to empty my mind. I read in the bible and think on what I read. I write a poem. If there is time, I write in my journal as well. Some days these things come easily. Other days, it's a struggle. I don't want to do it. My brain is flat. I am uninspired. Surely, I tell myself, skipping a day won't hurt.

And then I bear down, and I write anyway. I pray anyway. I journal anyway.

This makes me, I am told, "prolific". Perhaps that is so. I don't really measure that, or measure myself against what others do. What I do know is what it does for me. It keeps me sane. It is, I think, why discipline is important. Because when we are in places where the world beats us up, having that discipline keeps us alive at some level. even when I don't want to be, even though the depression tells me to surrender. And I have learned, that sometimes, simply having that discipline, opens us up to produce wonderful things that not only keep us sane, but helps others in their own struggles as well.

It has been, for me, a year of losses. I lost my mother. I lost my father. I ended a long relationship, which was also a deep loss.

Other things too were losses in this year, week after week, month after month. It has been unrelenting and I won't lie and say I did well with it. I have felt battered.

I survived it. That is all. And I kept writing, painting, photographing, preaching. Habit. Discipline. I often felt my work was not so good, but I kept at it. At times, I have been told, it was quite good, but I have had trouble sorting it out, the good from the bad. I just kept at the things that help me sort stuff out, rarely feeling things were sorting out, but being aware that somewhere down there, deep inside, it was.

I am not saying nothing went well, that there were no joys in my life. There were plenty. But as soon as I began to feel I could breath again, another loss would rock my world. There were days, lots of them, that I just wanted to crawl into a hole, stop taking my depression medicine, stop fighting for sanity and sleep away my existence. But good habits kept me going. Discipline kept me going. I did my creative work. I did my work work. I did my mental emotional work.

Discipline. I hate it. I love it.

One of those disciplines, and maybe the best and most important of all, is savoring the good. No matter how small. Sun on my face in the fall. A perfect cup of tea. A quiet conversation with friends. Petting the cat that isn't mine but lives on my back porch. A hug. Deep conversation. Small things compared the sense of loss that cudgeled me so brutally this year. But if savored, if mindfully savored and held close and gratitude spoken out loud for each one, they take on an amazing power. A healing power so strong you would not imagine it could be housed in such a small package.

And it can't be, unless we're mindful enough, disciplined enough, to claim them.

I am not going to pretend it is an easy discipline. If it was, we'd all be able to do it. But it does work. God tells us to do it. Buddha tells us to do it. Other religious and spiritual traditions tell us to do it.

And believers in each of those traditions spend countless days and weeks and months and years trying to learn how. Obviously it's not in our DNA. It takes work. But the work is not hard. The discipline is hard.

Why? Because we live in a world of distractions. An instant world. And we want instant results. Magic pills.

There are no magic pills. I have learned that in my own life and in following the lives of others in my life. There is discipline in small things. Discipline that develops the habits that carry us in good times and bad. Disciplines best learned when life is not a maelstrom, to prepare us for when it is. Each act is not hard – stringing them together in the midst of distractions, even when we don't want to, is hard.

We are so busy looking for the dramatic change, the amazing discovery, the one big thing that can change our lives, but honestly, I don't think it's there. It's made in small steps. Tiny disciplines. Persistence more than talent or magic.

Part of me finds that encouraging. Knowing the small things make a difference. I'm nothing special. But I can do small things. But part of me hates knowing this., Because the gig is up. It's up to me.

And so I take a deep breath. And another. And begin again. There's a new poem to write somewhere. A song to sing. I am tired. I don't want to do it.

But I'm going to. Cursing and screaming and singing all the way

Tom

ISOLATION IS THE ENEMY

Most of my life I have felt like I was on the inside, looking out. Looking out at what the rest of the world was feeling, what they were seeing, what they were experiencing. I rarely felt things the same way others did, or at least not on the same time. I rarely felt the level of joy that other people seemed to feel. I rarely had the same passion at my disposal that other people had. I absolutely sucked at small talk. (I still do.) .

Looking back, I suspect I was in some state of depression most of my life, certainly through most of my adulthood, likely some in college, perhaps even as a child. Unfortunately for me, I didn't realize it until l was around fifty. By then, my whole life had crashed around me, and I went to get help. But before then, I never saw it.

Depression, I have learned, is very sneaky. A lot of times it doesn't show up in the way it is portrayed in our culture. I was rarely "blue". I got things done. In fact, I was really, really productive. I laughed. I had relationships. People have told me that I made it look easy.

That is due to my mom, I think. She had a "never let 'em see you sweat" attitude to life. "People don't need to know your struggles" is a phrase that rings in my head even today, nearly two years after her death. And people rarely did see her sweat, despite a life as full of struggle as anyone else's. Ask people about my mom and they will talk about her graciousness, her poise, her kindness.

None of that was fake, but none of it was as easy as it appeared on the surface. She worked hard, and often with deep conflict just to get through her life. That was part of her magic, that she could live that graciously, despite all it took for her to do so.

The older I get, the more I realize how that way of thinking became my own. In fact, it pretty much became all of my siblings way of living.

When my own life came undone, I did something that I needed to do for myself. I needed to understand why, and how long things had been unraveling. I needed to see what others saw. So for nearly a year I visited with friends, people from church, past pastors and confidants. I didn't tell them anything. "Tell me," I simply said "What you saw when you saw me and my marriage."

I was surprised at the answers. It was eye opening, both in terms of what people did see, and what they did not. I appeared to be fine… Until I wasn't. I never felt like I was hiding things. But I am sure my mom's refrain, "People don't need to know your struggles." was ringing in my head somewhere.

I realized too, how my father's anger played into not talking about my emotions. He had trouble with emotions too. Now I realize that like me, he was slow to process them. Unlike me, that made him angry, and he didn't want to hear about feelings or emotions. I was blasted for mine on a regular basis.

And that made it hard for me to talk about them. From time to time in my life, I have had a person to had great patience with me as I worked out feelings in my head. But most people really don't want to hear our struggles. We have a societal ritual. You ask "How are you." I answer "Fine".

I worked through most of that. I came to a place, with a lot of help, where I could finally talk through and find my emotions. I came to a place where I could manage my depression pretty well. And, when I have a rough day, few people notice. (Thanks Mom!). I learned to live within the limitations of my slow emotional processing, and even to make it work for me.

Most people don't want to know my struggles. Mom was actually right about that. They don't need or want to know that each and every morning I wake up, I have to force myself to get out of bed. Not just tiredness or laziness, it's the depression lying to me that there's no reason to get going, that no one will notice or care if I don't. They never see the battle.

Or, that I win it each morning. And that first victory sets me up to win the next few victories. Why do I meditate, pray, and write poetry every morning? There's no virtue in it. It doesn't make me a morning person. No, I do it because that victory of going to God and asking for help, that victory of stilling my mind, that victory of letting my emotion run through me and turning it into words, into poems, sets me and my wayward mind on the right path for the day.

It's my "big mo" And most days it lasts me all day long. I run on the inertia of that string of small victories.

I still feel on the inside looking out. Sixty years of living in that place have taught me how to manage that too. I surround myself with extroverts, and their energy is contagious. I have learned it's OK to be quiet, to be a watcher, to be the introvert I am. I have learned that it's OK to silently fight my battles, as long as I have a couple of people with the patience to listen, who understand that yes, I struggle, but no, they don't have to fix it. Just love me through it.

No, most people don't want or need to know. But some do. Some do, a lot.

And so, I have learned, it is OK to share in in a bigger sense. To talk about it when it's an appropriate time to do so. To write about it. Not everyone will listen. A lot won't care. But some will.

Because, I have learned – most of us who struggle, with depression, with PTSD, with remnants of child abuse, or whatever the struggle we have, tend to do it alone. We tend to think the struggle is ours alone. And in that isolation, we weaken. Slowly. Steadily. And we end up a mess. We collapse. We recluse. We screw up relationships.

And that is so self destructive. We need each other. We need to know we are not alone. We need to know others are fighting the same battles, sometimes winning, sometimes losing, but still, battling. Courage is found in others around us. Strength is found in others around us.

It's not whining. It's not complaining. It's not …… Pick your negative. It's selective sharing that can help people. You have no idea how many people, as a result of my simply saying "I fight depression" have ended up having long talks with me, and ending up getting help.

They are still fighting their battles, but they are no longer fighting them alone.

Some feel like admitting their struggles is a bad thing. That it makes them somehow, weak. I say it's just the opposite. Admitting our weakness and getting help and battling the demons, with help, makes us stronger. Isolation makes us weaker.

Let me repeat that: Isolation makes us weaker. Isolation is the enemy.

That is not how we tend to think when we are in the midst of our struggles. But it is the truth.

And the truth, my friends, will set you free.

The battles won't end. The struggles will not be over. But when we take on allies. When we call on our God and when we find those who have traveled the same journey; when we share our truth and march into the fray together... We win.

Be well. Travel wisely,

Tom

WHY

I had a rough morning this morning. That's OK. I have about 300 or so of them a year. It's my normal. I know how to push myself past the depression and get going. It's a routine that serves me well. If you have read this far, you already know what that routine is. Some time in the bible. Some time meditating. Some time writing poetry. About 30 – 45 minutes or so each morning.

It's not gone after that, but it's pushed back into its cave and I can go on. Some days, it behaves very nicely, stays in the cave and I don't hear a whimper. Other days it seems to resent being marginalized and I can hear it muttering threats all day. But pretty much, it stays put while I get about my business.

I was having lunch with my friend Jon the other day and he asked me if it helped me writing about my depression. And the answer is, yes, it does. But that's only one reason I write about it.

It is no secret to anyone who knows me, or who has spent much time reading on my blog, that I use poetry less as art or literature, than as a way to sort out things in my head and heart. The truth is that I am often not very glib with the language of feelings. There was a point, about a decade and a half ago, when I was downright stifled in my ability to say what I feeling.

The hows of how I got there are not that important. The fact that I had gotten there is. In a way, I liken it to having had a stroke, only it affected my ability to feel and express my feelings. I practically had to relearn how to recognize and relate my feelings all over again.

Thank goodness for persistent therapists. Mine pushed me, twisted me, turned me inside out, made me look at a lot of uncomfortable stuff, and we came to the place where we recognized that part of the problem was my depression. We did all the things you do to learn to battle depression, but she also put me on kind of a rehab, helping me regain my ability to fully recognize and express not just the basic feelings, but the more subtle ones. Getting back to poetry was part of that process. It's still part of how I sort my world out.

In my house, particularly with my Dad, the "D" word was never used. And therapists? Forget about it. Therapists were for Hollywood and whackos. Not us real people. So when I started going to one, well it wasn't exactly encouraged. I kept it quiet. But I pounded away at it. Week after week for three and a half years. And for another eighteen months or so after I moved from Virginia to Vermont. I still check in now and again to make sure I am on good paths, or to help me deal with anything that has the potential to be overwhelming.

I kept it quiet unless someone came to me dealing with the same things. Then I talked about my journey and my struggles and how getting the tools to fight it can change life and make it a joy again. And it made a difference. And so, I began to talk about it now and again in my church, when it fit. And it made a difference. One or two people at a time, but it made the uncomfortableness of talking about it worthwhile.

I wrote about it in my blog for the first time a few months ago. It was after a discussion with someone here in my neck of the woods where I had talked about how Depression doesn't stop you. There's millions of us functioning just fine thank you. You'd never know we were battling it because we don't fit the stereotype of the person that can't get out of bed and barely functions. Not us. We're taking the kids to ball games, leading committees at church and in the community, are strong, capable co-workers, but…. and here's the but… it's damned hard. And people don't get that. So I wrote my first piece.

And I was flat out stunned at the response. I don't know what you people did or who you passed it on to, but the response and readership was many, many times what my blog normally has. I got all kinds of notes and emails (I don't get very many on a normal day.). And I realized that there are a lot more of us in this battle than I knew. A LOT more.

And I found that somehow, having someone put it out there, helps. So I've written a few more pieces, as I see or learn something about my own situation that might resonate. And true to that first one. It generally does.

So the second part of the answer to Jon's question is yes, it helps me write about it because it matters to people. It evidently helps some of you reading this, even if it just assures you that you are not alone.

One of the things I think most of us want out of life is to make a difference. It doesn't seem to matter where we live, what our religion is, or what level of society we come from, we want to change things around us for the better. We want our lives to have meaning. And if you can turn your own suffering into something that makes a difference, then that gives the suffering and the work to overcome it, value. It takes something lousy, painful and hard, and gives it meaning.

And so I write.

It will never be comfortable. It will never be easy. But it's part of my war. It helps me. And hopefully, it helps some others as well. I am closing in on a small book's worth of essays and poems on depression and I'll likely compile it all in the fall. My hope is that I can portray it the way I see it – that depression is a handicap, not a mark of being less a person, or less strong. Hardly that. It's a battle. And I want to go from being a drudge grunt in the battle, which is where I've been most of the past decade, to a joyous warrior, on the front line, charging into battle.

Come join me. You can, you know.

Tom

FEAR

I see it in business, with clients. Just a couple of weeks ago I had a consultation with a client who told me, actually told me, "I know everything you've given me is true. I know your path is solid and would work. But I can't do it." (Excuse me while I pull my last hair out.)

I see it in everyday life, with people battling depression, or other emotional issues, or relational issues, or, or, or. Such a list! I see it in my work as a part-time pastor. I rarely have to tell anyone what they should do to deal with their problems. They already know. And they already have their list of reasons they "can't".

On the drive back hone from a few days off in Mystic, CT, I thought back to my own life. There have been times I knew I had to do something, or stop doing something, or get help, and I resisted it. Hard. Really, really hard. Looking back, I had trouble understanding why. What madness made me think I was so different, so unique that I could ignore proven ways to get well? What pride made me ignore what had I knew had to be done? What fear held me back?

Looking at myself, I realized that the last one was the big barrier. Fear. Fear of change. Fear that I was weak? Fear of what people would think?.Fear that an admission of weakness or flaws would make me less of a person?. Fear of hurting or inconveniencing someone? Fear of the work involved? (Because often it's hard. Really hard). Fear of failure? Fear of success (and what that might mean in terms of change, loss, or challenge)?

All of the above, in my case.

One of the things my few years of counseling taught me is that I am not nearly as unique as I would like to think I am. That when I have issues or problems to overcome, more times than not, plenty of people have been through the same thing, suffered the same thing, battled the same thing. And more times than not, listening to their paths helps me find my own, even when it's scary.

And it often is.

In my case, I think I had to hit rock bottom emotionally and spiritually to rethink the fear. I seriously don't recommend that rock bottom place for anyone. I had to get to a place where I could realize that when I think fear is a reason for not doing something, I am generally wrong. To learn that pushing past the fear is the path to not just growth, but to something better.

That's been my experience, anyway. That better always, ALWAYS, lives on the other side of fear. Does that make me fear less? Nope. But it does give me courage. It's allowed me to overcome a lot of fears. It will get past more of them.

In my sermon this past week, we were reading from John 5:1-9. Jesus is talking to a cripple and he asks the cripple a question: "Do you want to be healed?". That question haunted me all week. It haunted me like a ghost when I was the shipyard in Mystic. It haunted me on the long drive back. Because I still fight demons. Because so many people I love, or I know have battles, hurts, scars, and challenges that they have lived with for years, for decades, for lifetimes. Why?

Fear. The very thing that is our barrier, I have learned, is also part of our path to where we want to be.

I wish we spent more time teaching kids, and teaching ourselves, how to attack fear. How to make it the enemy. And most importantly, how to realize that just on the other side of that fear, lies all the things we want in life.

Do I have answers? Not completely. I think the answers are there, but they are often unique to each person. Or at least that is what I have learned the past few years as I have managed, coached and mentored people. There does not seem to be a once size fits all answer to fear.

But there is a universal first step. To admit it. To name it. We don't like admitting fear because it makes us feel weak. It makes us feel vulnerable. But it is the start, I believe, to saying "Yes, I want to be healed. I want to get past this. I want to be…… better."

Once we admit the fear. Once we claim it and give it a name, then the solution is there. Because others have been there. Remember, we are more alike than we are unique. And once we find those others, we have a path past our beautiful fear.

Of course then, the games up. We can't hide from it. The question becomes the same one Jesus asked the cripple : Do we want to get well?"

Which is scary in itself, isn't it?

Yep, the gig's up.

Tom

TOM THE BESERKER

I went into therapy about a little more than decade ago because I felt like I was coming apart. A couple of months after I began, my life really did fall apart.

Regular readers already know my story. I fell into a black place. Depression on steroids. You know, the kind of depression you read about where you feel paralyzed, where you can't get going, can't make yourself do things, where you struggle to get going in the morning. Yeah, I was pretty much the poster child. Cue fetal position.

Some people ask me if I have "triggers" for depression, things that send me into a dark place. I've spent a lot of time thinking about that because sometimes you live with something so long that you don't really think about it. It just is. As I have thought about it, and looked back, I've come to realize that it's not that simple.

There's no "one size fits all" way to deal with depression. It seems to be part art and part science and part war and it takes a while to sort out how much of which it takes to beat the beast back.

There's the science of course. We know that depression is a disease or syndrome – it's physical. Most of us have a mix of chemicals and hormones that keep us thinking and feeling in healthy ways. For a few of us, that mix gets out of whack, and our brains begin to lie to us, tell us things are bad, that we aren't loved, that we can't get going, that it's useless, that we are useless, unlovable, not enough, that life is hopeless.

And our brain, wonder that it is, is pretty stupid. If our mix of chemicals and hormone tell us it's hopeless, it believes us. It becomes reality.

To get past it, first we have to get our chemical mix right. That's why we take medication. (I call mine "happy pills" even though that's not really what they do.). For me, and most of us, it doesn't fix much, but it at least makes it possible for us to do the other half of what we have to do without the chemicals in our head sabotaging us.

You see, that brain of ours has been lying to us for years, maybe decades. And when we tell ourselves something over and over and over, that dumb brain of ours believes it. It becomes OUR reality. So the second part of the journey is to start re-teaching our brain. That's what therapy does. It helps us find the lies we've been telling ourselves, the things we have been hiding from or have put into some closet trying to avoid the pain or the confusion, the things that have told us what a useless piece of humanity we are, or have paralyzed us.

That's actually pretty hard work. Really hard work. I've had to do physical therapy for injuries and that kind of physical work HURTS. It takes time. The progress is slow. It's frustrating.

Therapy is harder.

But it's an essential part of the process. adndoh so worth it. And if we see it through, with a good counselor, it can work wonders. On depression, and a host of other things. I used to laugh at shrinks and the whole idea, a belief inherited from my father, who had a disdain for such things, thinking that it was all mumbo-jumbo. I am an evangelist now.

So, with all that background (Sorry, I tend to wander, and nothing is simple so I tend to tell too many back stories. Sigh.), let me answer the question, or at least begin to.

If we depressed folk are on medication, then hopefully the chemicals in our brain are all nice and balanced. And if we're doing the therapy part, we're making progress in undoing the lies our brain has been telling itself. All is good… except.

Except our brains are not a stable thing. No, I am not saying we're all psychotic, but only that things change. As we age, as we live with more or less stress, the chemical mix may change. So even with my "happy pills", I may not always be in balance. As long as life goes on with normal ups and down my depression is pretty much under control. Until it isn't. Until something changes.

That something can be a trigger. Or it can be chemical. Or it can be a wearing down because of stress or self-neglect (We depressed folks are notoriously bad at self-care.). It can be fast, or (more commonly) it can sneak up on us while we are not watching.

That's where the third factor comes in. Anger.

First, let me tell you that I hate anger. HATE it. As a kid, I bore my father's temper with fear and trepidation. He could totally paralyze me with his anger, and for much of my life, and I do mean most of it, anger had that same effect – it paralyzed me. I hated it in others. And I hated it when I felt it, sure somehow that I was bad when I showed anger. It took years and years for me to move past that point. I still go, very, very briefly into that fight or flight place when someone is unloading on me , but it's crazy brief now. It just doesn't have that effect any more.

And maybe, more importantly, I have learned how to use my anger. Like a sword. Like a shield. Not on myself. Not (often) on others. But on my depression.

I have declared depression to be my enemy. It has, after all, all the elements of a good villain. It lies. It is controlling, but always negatively. It's sneaky. It is destructive. I had a good life before my depression and my depression has cost me a lot of years without that good life. I don't hate well, but I will tell you this. I HATE my depression.

Hate is very valuable in this context. It gives me an energy to fight depression even when I am tired, beat up, worn out, don't want to and would just like to give in. But anger, well used, has a power and energy that I often lack on my own. It is my arch nemesis. Like Moriarty to Sherlock Holmes. Always there, in the shadows, lurking, waiting.

This is not being mad. We get mad at people and it flares and goes away. This is an abiding, fiery, deep-from-my-soul anger. My depression took a lot from me, and I have taken it back. I fight to defend what I have reclaimed. Fighting and anger are still not comfortable to me, never will be. I love peace. I love low stress.

But anger fuels me every day. And without it, I would be riding much more of a roller coaster with my depression than I do now. Anger puts me on my guard, on the offensive and gives both my medicine and my cognitive work (therapy) a fighting chance. Because it IS a fight.

Is it right for everyone, this anger? I don't know. It works for me. Others who do well with their depression tell me that it works for them too.

A lot of us who are open about our depression, talk about how we suffer depression. Some manage it. A few of us talk about battling it. I don't want to suffer it. I am not even satisfied managing or battling it. I want to be a frigging berserker, horned Viking helmet, shining broadsword, steel shield and all, screaming like a madman as I charge it each day, eyes ablaze and full of fury

Quietly of course. Don't want to wake the neighbors.

GOOBLETY GOOP

Some of you regular readers may have caught on to it. Certainly my friends and family have. Something has been "not right" with me for a couple of months.

My depression was worse, which is no big deal. It does that some time. I have a strategy for that. (Thank you O wonderful Therapists in my life.). But I was also having a hard time thinking, which is a problem since so much of my work involves thinking.

My short term memory was gone. (Fortunately, I have a habit of writing most things down, but still….) Now, I know I am not a young guy anymore, but the last I heard senility tends to creep in slowly, almost unnoticed. This was like someone hit a switch.

I got stuff done. I met my deadlines. My clients seemed happy with my work. I got sermons written and delivered. My kid and my cat got fed regularly. But it was such a slog.

I made some changes. I have permission from my doc to up my depression meds. I normally live on a low dose, but I am allowed to max it out if I think I need it. So I notched it up. Nothing. I changed my diet a bit. I began to get out more and exercise more. Nada. Zip. I felt like I was living in a viscous fog.

A couple of days at Cape Cod helped my mood. Of course it did. Long empty beaches. Ocean and horizons. Fresh air. No deadlines.

No responsibilities. Seafood. How could that not help a man's mood?

But it didn't really fix anything.

So I have ploughed through. It's not been much fun, and mostly, for me, life is fun. Even work is mostly fun. But not the past few months.

I have become old enough that every time I meet with my doctor, he begins "In a man your age....." So I began to think, maybe this is what old age is like. I'm only sixty, but maybe this is just what happens. If it is, it sucks.

A few days ago, I was cruising through my facebook feed and one of my friends had posted something about statins and depression. Evidently, the article said, there is a strong link between the two. As I read the article it was like reading a list of my symptoms. So I dove into it more. Article after article. Study after study. I killed off the afternoon reading.

Why so interested? Because it was just after the doc put me on Statins for some borderline high cholesterol that I went all fog brained. I didn't make the connection then because... well... I was fog brained.

I know docs hate people that self diagnose. But I felt like it was worth a go. I was after all, just a notch high. And it was a precaution because I am diabetic, not because he felt I had a real problem. (Yeah, Yeah, we humans can justify anything can't we?)

I decided to stop the statins for a week. Just a week, to see. So that first night, I didn't take one with my bedtime reading, and got up the next morning. Bada bing. Bada boom. I was my old self again. Alert. Ready to charge into my day. Singing to myself (OK, that might not be an improvement.)

A couple of days into it, it appears that was it. I called my doc this morning. He's OK with it. And boy do I like being back.

What's the lesson? (I always think things have a lesson. It's a character flaw.)

One, if something changes quickly, there's a reason. Normal aging is a slow thing. Sudden changes are something going whacko. Don't write yourself off, keep probing and poking for an answer. This is true for physical things. Emotional things. And spiritual things.

Second. Keep probing. Keep trying. There are generally answers out there, but the body of knowledge is so huge that we can't expect the doctors to know everything about everything. Think about it – a zillion ailments, each with a dozen possible causes, treated by a dozen different drugs, and 30 patients a day, all different. The matrix of possibilities are huge. They are great, most of them, but in the end, you know you, and we have to take some responsibility to push things forward, or we get lost.

A good life is worth the extra effort to help make it happen.

One good thing that comes out of something like this, and I have noticed it other times when I've been seriously ill or injured. When you do come back, you have a renewed sense of gratitude for the good things in life. Something as simple as thinking becomes something to cheer about. And gratitude is good for the soul.

For my soul, at least.

.

Tom

THE SUMMER PHOENIX

Make no mistake,
it is a battle of attrition,
of will and willingness
to fight back,
to claim each golden step
as if it were the last,
and fight on,
to refuse

to suffer.

For suffering
is passive.
You have already lost
when that is your choice.

But battling!
It is gritty, not glorious,
but there is always the chance
of victory.
It is full of possibility,
a refusal to surrender,
to go down perhaps, but
always to rise again
and again,

the summer phoenix,
a light in the distance
despite the relentless dark
that cannot stand
as long as you, do.

About this poem.

I was discussing depression with a reporter this morning, and I spoke about battling depression vs suffering depression. When we battle, we can win. We take part in our own victory. When we choose to simply suffer, we have already lost.

Me? I choose to be a warrior.

Tom

DANCING WITH DEPRESSION

There is no final chapter.

That, ultimately, is the lesson of my depression.

It's a battle. Just that. Some of us become casualties, bodies on the battlefield, conquered by chemicals in our brain, conquered by a society that blindly looks down on the depressed and lives mostly in ignorance.

Some of us are the walking wounded. Stumbling through the battlefield, able to function, but only just. We wear our wounds, but mostly hidden away, afraid of the scorn or dismissiveness of the world around us, unwilling or unable to take any more injury.

Some of us are warriors. Pissed off dervishes who fight it day in and day out, determined to fight back, even knowing that the term victory does not apply. At best we hold the line and push it back a little. We function well, but in mostly in secret, determined to have what society calls a normal life despite the wounds.

I've been all three. That is the story of my last decade and a half. It has not been a story that runs in a straight line like a Disney movie. It is an up and down ragged roller coaster.

It is a dance. A tango, with its mix of love and aggression. It has been at times ugly, at times exhilaration, at times a slog.

I have said it before in these essays – some of the people who fight depression are the most courageous people I know. They fight a battle no one sees, that no one appreciates with, and often, even though they should not have to, they fight it alone. They fight it in a world that mostly dismisses it as the blues, or as some horrible flaw, that dismisses them rather than seeing them for what they are – people of courage.

The key word in all this is fight. Some people succumb to depression. It is simply too much. Some people struggle with it, surviving and little more. And some people fight it and come close to a victory.

I wish I had wisdom about how you move from succumbing to struggling to fighting. Even though I have made the journey, I have no magic. I have no secret.

I do know this though – we don't do it alone. We need help, just like a man on the battle field with a mangled leg needs help, so do we. We don't get out on our own. In my case, I had two loving pastors that held me up, I had two therapists, one in Virginia and another here in Vermont when I moved, that forced me through the process of healing. I had family, who even if they didn't fully get it, hung in with me as I crawled back.

The temptation is to crawl into yourself. That feels like the safe thing to do. Your brain is whispering it's lies about your worth and value and ability and alone in your hole seems the only safe place to get away. Some people line their hole with alcohol or drugs or other numbing agents. Some simply crawl in and sit.

It feels safe, but it is not. What saves us is help. Help that helps us stand and helps us learn to see the lies for what they are. Help that reminds us of our value, that gives us weapons. It feels unsafe at first. It feels dangerous and it's not an easy path.

No battle is.

But it is the path back. The path to warrior-hood. The road to almost normal. And it never ends.

That's right, it never ends. We age. Our body chemistry changes. The medications we took at the beginning of the journey have to be adjusted. Things trigger us. Depression is a sneaky opponent, often lying low, hiding in the bushes, waiting for a time when you are weak or unaware then pouncing like the Indians on Custer. Without diligence, the path from succumbing to struggling to warrior status can go backwards.

This too is why we don't want to be fighting this alone. As the people around us understand the nature of our enemy, they can sometimes see our slide better than we can. They can point out what's happening before we've lost another battle. They can give us support.

And we can do the same for others. You see, we are aware of the danger like no one else. We are in a better place to reach out to others that fight depression because we "get" it. We have fought past the shame and know the nature of our enemy in a way others do not.

Depending on the stats you read, roughly one out of ten people are dealing with depression. Think of that as you go through your day. Look around. Count, 1,2,3,4,5,6,7,8,9,10 as people pass through your life. And when you do, realize one of those people are like us, fighting the same battles. Having lived that battle, we can be particular help. We help people realize they are not alone, and that things can get better. They can get less hard.

And we, you and I, the walking wounded, the silent warriors, can help.

Helping not only makes a difference to whoever we are reaching out to, it gives our battle purpose. And sometimes we need purpose when we are in the midst of it. We need something beyond ourselves. Because it keeps us from being isolated.

But the battle never ends. We are always at risk. The enemy is always there. There is no cure. Only the battle.

For me, sharing is part of my battle. It is my battle song, sung as dive into my day, sung as I swing my sword and keep the enemy at bay, and at the end of the day, when I look back at what I have done, who I have helped, the love I have felt and the love I have experienced, I sing even louder. It does not matter if I sing well. It only matters that I sing. I think of it as one of those war movies, when, outnumbered and out manned, the smaller, about to be destroyed army begins, first with one man, then another, then the entire army takes up the hymn and charges to victory.

This book is my wavering song. Will you sing with me? Today might not be the final chapter, but I want it to be a glorious one. For me and for you. Put on your warrior shoes, and dance.

It drives depression crazy, dancing.

Tom

DONE. NOT DONE

I woke up this morning flat-lined. Dull. Dark.

Pretty normal for me.

And *that* being my normal? It makes me mad. I wasn't always like this. I used to be bright and obnoxiously cheerful in the mornings. Yeah, I was one of those. You'd probably have hated me in the mornings.

But today is my normal and has been for a lot of years. So it takes a little work. Even more, for me, it takes a bit of anger. And so, after laying in the bed for a few minutes not wanting to get up, whispers in my head telling me it doesn't matter whether I get up or not.

Lies. And lies make me angry. Myself telling myself lies makes me angriest.

And so I got up. I put my feet on the ground. I said my ritual morning phrase "It's Showtime!" and started my day. I performed my sanity rituals. I pet the cat. I had a conversation with the woman I love. I had some coffee. Actually, I had a lot of coffee. I got to work. It's mid day as I write this, and I've done some good work. My clients will be pleased. I'm looking forward to the afternoon. More work. Some time in the garden. A long walk.

None of that probably sounds very exciting. But for me, it's another victory. I win them almost every day.

Depression has made me stronger. It has taught me to fight. It has taught me that life is worth fighting for. It has taught me that I am stronger than I ever imagined, by making me weaker than I ever imagined. It has made me more empathetic. It has made me more forgiving of myself and others. It has taught me discipline. It has taught me compassion for others.

And I still hate it.

By now you know. I often liken it to a battle. But at times, I think of it more as a tango, that dance which is a mix of passion and aggression. Love and hate and strange exotic music.

This morning, I finished my book on depression. This book you are reading this very moment. Over the next week I will begin to format it for publication.

What next, someone asked me this morning. Will I stop writing about it? Have I had my say?

Not likely.

Everything in life has layers. Very little that happens in life ever really goes away. It hides in closets and under our rugs waiting to show up again. And certainly depression doesn't go away. It's a dragon in a cage, ready to escape and ravage our internal landscapes at any moment. One doesn't walk away from that. Not after you've been burned a few times. I'll continue to write.

This little book is my experience. It's not a how-to manual. There are plenty of those already out there. It's not a substitute for getting real help. It is simply my story. If you have been reading it and fight depression yourself, I hope you have been reminded that you are not alone. There's a lot of us. I hope you have been reminded that the battle can be fought and won, even if the war goes on. Joy can be yours again, but it doesn't come easy and it doesn't come when we fight it alone.

If you are a reader without depression, I hope you've gotten some insight to those you know who are in the midst of their own battle. Their battles will be different than mine in some ways, but know that they are indeed fighting a battle, a war, and those who, like me, have fought their way to a good life are some of the most courageous people you will ever know. And those who are overcome by it have been overcome by a particularly vile and persistent foe. Hopefully you have a little more understanding.

And me? I'll continue. I am not content to just survive. I want joy for myself. And I want it for you.

We deserve it, you and I.

Tom

ABOUT THE AUTHOR

Tom Atkins is a poet, writer, painter and photographer living in West Pawlet Vermont. He's also a part time pastor of two small Methodist Churches in Southwest Vermont, and has a 30 year history in the broadcast technology world. He is part of the John Maxwell Team of consultants, coaches and public speakers.

This is his fourth book. Beyond the work he does for clients, Atkins keeps up three blogs, a small yard, one cat and two pretty grown up kids.

He keeps himself busy.

Web site: www.quarryhouse.us

Other Books by Tom Atkins

Love in a Minor Key (poems and photographs)

Madman's Courage (poems)

The Wisdom Letters (Poems and Essays)